Spotted Owlets

written by VICTORIA MILES
illustrated by ELIZABETH GATT

ORCA BOOK PUBLISHERS

Father owl is hunting for the family and Mother owl is waiting outside the nest. She is calling *hoo . . . hoo-hoo . . . hoo . . .* to her young.

One little owlet peers further out of the tree. He turns his head and looks about. He has never been outside the tree trunk before. He stretches his wings, steps forward and tumbles . . .

wings flapping, all the way down to the forest floor.

Mother owl is watching him. She is ready to swoop down and help, but she can see that he is safe—just a little dizzy for the moment.

High above in the nest, his sister clings to the edge of the hole with her talons and stretches. She too steps forward and falls . . .

to a branch below.

Now that they have left the nest, they will not go back inside it again.

This climbing is very hard work for the little owlet. After taking a few steps upwards he is tired, so he stops and clings tightly to the bark of the tree with his talons. Bracing himself with his wings against the tree trunk, he takes a rest.

Mother is still watching.

The owlet begins to climb again. This time it is a bit easier, and he uses his beak to help pull himself up . . . up . . .

all the way to his sister! They perch there together, sharing the branch.

Mother turns her head as Father owl sweeps down beside her. He passes the food he has brought for the owlets from his beak to hers.

The owlets are really excited now. Over and over they use their high voices to call out *suweet!* . . . *suweet!* . . . *suweet!* . . .

Mother hops down to their perch and divides the meal between them. With a couple of gulps each, the owlets make their dinner disappear.

Every night, when the forest is very dark, the little owlets move about. They stretch and flap their wings—getting ready for their first flight—and they take steps back and forth on the limbs of the tree.

When they fall, and they sometimes do, they climb back up the tree to a safe branch.

Northern spotted owls (*Strix occidentalis caurina*) are an uncommon resident in old-growth forests of the Pacific Northwest — virtually the only type of forest in which they occur. They are dependent upon these older forests for food, shelter, nesting sites and concealment from larger birds of prey. The future of northern spotted owls depends heavily upon the preservation of sufficient tracts of the ancient forests where they still exist.

Without the research on the spotted owl performed by Dr. Eric Forsman, Dave Dunbar and their colleagues, this book would not have been possible.

Text copyright © 1993 Victoria Miles
Illustration copyright © 1993 Elizabeth Gatt

Publication assistance provided by The Canada Council.
All rights reserved.

Orca Book Publishers
PO Box 5626, Station B
Victoria, BC Canada
V8R 6S4

Orca Book Publishers
Box 3028, 1574 Gulf Road
Point Roberts, WA   USA
98281

Canadian Cataloguing in Publication Data
Miles, Victoria, 1966 –
   Spotted owlets

   ISBN 1-55143-004-5

   I. Spotted owl – Juvenile literature.   I.
Gatt, Elizabeth, 1951 –   II. Title.
QL696.S83M54 1993   j598.9'7   C93-091563

Design by Christine Toller
Printed and bound in Hong Kong